Economics of Pharmaceutical Development

Economics of Pharmaceutical Development

A review of modern valuation theories

Giampiero Favato

Writers Club Press

San Jose New York Lincoln Shanghai

Economics of Pharmaceutical Development
A review of modern valuation theories

Writers Club Press
an imprint of iUniverse.com, Inc.

For information address:
iUniverse.com, Inc.
5220 S 16th, Ste. 200
Lincoln, NE 68512
www.iuniverse.com

ISBN: 0-595-19804-X

Printed in the United States of America

CONTENTS

Table of figures vii

Introduction ix

Current inefficiencies in the R&D process. 1

Evidence based modelling of drug development. 5

Modelling Risk and Value of R&D Projects. 9

Cost-benefit analysis. 13

Management Information and Decision Sciences. 19

Parametric Cost Models to estimate research cost. 31

Financial and Risk Analysis Models 41

Integration of NPV and Risk Analysis. 45

EVA®: Driver of Market Value. 49

Real Options 57

Conclusions and Future Research 65

Bibliography 67

TABLE OF FIGURES

Figure 1: Evolution of valuation models x

Figure 2: Evidence based Time-Cost model
of Pharmaceutical R&D 7

Figure 3: Influence diagram. 10

Figure 4: Probability of the possible outcomes of an event. 11

Figure 5: Common risks related to Pharmaceutical R&D 12

Figure 6: CER Development Process 35

Figure 7: Expected NPV distribution
as indication for project risk. 47

Figure 8: Drivers of project to project EVA® variability. 52

Figure 9: Abandon Options in Pharmaceutical R&D 58

Figure 10: Value of options in Pharmaceutical R&D 60

Figure 11: Decision tree. 62

Figure 12: Investment opportunities using
Option Pricing (Luehrman 1998) 63

Figure 13: Suggested financial models   (Bode Greuel 2000) 64

Figure 14: Decision Making tools (Rahmani 1999). 66

INTRODUCTION

Over the last decade, the approach to strategic management of Drug Development has been progressively rationalised, in parallel to the development of financial and risk analysis quantitative models.

This book examines the evolution of R&D risk-adjusted models, arguing that financial evaluation has progressively moving away from deterministic quantitative analysis, in favour of non-linear, stochastic algorithms.

The relentless quest for capturing the value of Pharmaceutical Research will demand for a new emphasis on integration among disciplines and models.

The application of risk adjusted evaluation models to earlier stages of the discovery process is an important area for further research and value creation.

Figure 1: Evolution of valuation models

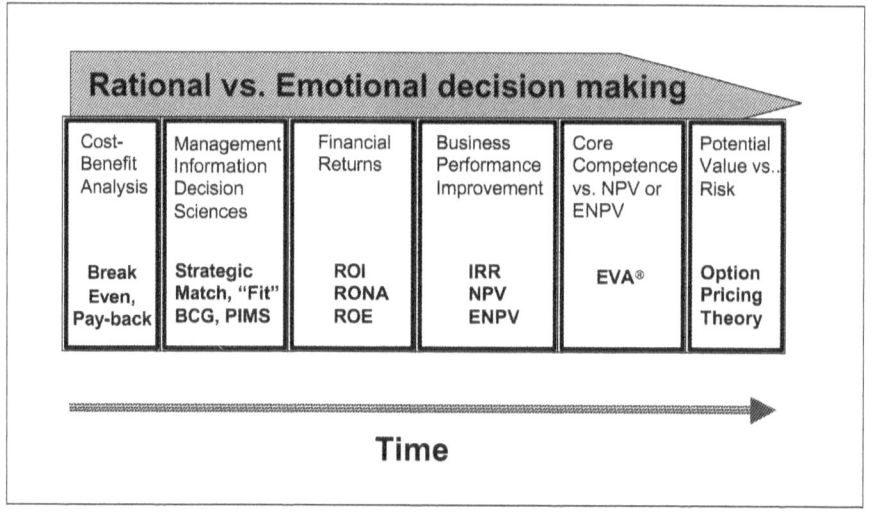

CURRENT INEFFICIENCIES IN THE R&D PROCESS.

The past two decades have seen radical changes to the pharmaceutical industry, with ever increasing competition pressuring the major companies to dramatically improve the productivity of their R&D departments in order to remain profitable. The increase in average R&D expenditure as a percentage of sales, from 12% in the early 1980s to nearly 20% by 1997, has adversely affected profitability levels in the pharmaceutical industry. However, this increased investment in R&D has not resulted in proportionally greater numbers of product approvals. Over the period 1985 to 1995, the four year rolling average of the number of world wide New Chemical Entity (NCE) approvals increased by approximately 20% whereas the investment in research is estimated to have increased by over 200% in the same period (Datamonitor 1997).

A number of factors have contributed to the inefficiencies which currently plague the research efforts of major pharmaceutical companies:

   □   The increase in research and development time for a drug candidate. The R&D time scale has lengthened markedly since 1960s, when the average time from initial investigation to product approval was 8 years, to the 1990s when this figure is over 15 years. This has two serious implications:

1

- The cost of development has increased markedly;
- The marketable patent life of approved products has decreased dramatically.

□ The high failure rates of drug candidates in pre-clinical and clinical research.

These two factors have led to the situation currently faced today, where expensive and unproductive R&D is failing to meet the needs of pharmaceutical companies who demand a steady, reliable stream of new products. The pharmaceutical industry cannot sustain the increases in R&D investment observed over the last two decades.

A key short-term goal of pharmaceutical companies is to reduce R&D expenditure without adversely affect output. Optimisation of stop-go decisions, leading to increased project and candidate shedding, was viewed as the key strategy to achieve this objective.

Without exception, industry experts believe that companies are pursuing more aggressive selection policies within the R&D process. Toxicology is viewed as the phase where increased project shedding is currently occurring. However, is felt that the balance will shift to a higher level of stringency in optimisation within the next decade. Lead generation and phase I clinical studies are other key stages where project shedding is improving the use of resources. The most expensive stages of the R&D process, phase II and phase III clinical studies, are perceived as the key areas where there is large scope for reduction over the next decade. Lead optimisation and generation are also likely to see reductions in expenditure, largely through the application of enabling technologies.

The enabling technologies of genomics, combinatorial chemistry and rationale drug design (molecular modelling, computer aided molecule design) are perceived as the key technologies which will allow greater success in drug discovery process over the next ten years. These technologies will improve the quality of candidate molecules, as they possess the following advantages:

☐ Genomics allow a greater diversity of drug targets to be identified. Although its potential has not been realised, experts view it as pivotal to improving innovation in the drug discovery process, and recognise the technology's potential for excellent return on investment over the next ten years, as it becomes viable.

☐ Combinatorial chemistry is considered to be the key driver towards reduced development time. Combinatorial chemistry can vastly decrease the time needed for lead generation and optimisation and it is considered one of the main stream for new investment in R&D.

☐ Rational drug design has the potential to greatly improve the selection of candidates for clinical trials, by improving accurate information on drug-target interactions and therefore optimising the structure of candidate molecules. By providing a starting structure for the generation of candidate molecules, rational drug design can complement combinatorial chemistry and thus improve the efficiency of lead generation and optimisation stages. Most importantly, analysis of molecular interactions increases the chances of successful in vivo activity and therefore improves product success rates in phase II and phase III clinical trials.

The three enabling technologies can thus act in concert to reduce time and improve efficiency in pre-clinical development, and maximise the chances of candidate success in clinical studies, leading to increased product approval rates.

Optimal stop-go decision in R&D process is receiving considerable attention as the single key driver to maximise the value of drug discovery. As well as reducing expenditure, increased project and product shedding reduces the ratio of unsuccessful to successful drug candidates. This would lead to obvious productivity improvements. More careful selection of projects requires strategic decision making, while candidate selection can benefit from the application of new technologies as mentioned above. Improved lead optimisation allows the selection of a limited number of candidates with greater chances of subsequent clinical success and reduces the number of products less likely to receive approval.

EVIDENCE BASED MODELLING OF DRUG DEVELOPMENT.

Reflecting on the limitations of prior research, mostly lacking of methodological structure, in 1999 the Author felt the need to generalise the timeline and the cost of the pharmaceutical R&D process by deriving a normally distributed model from secondary data. To satisfy the statistical condition, he struggled to get an appropriate database reporting a long enough developmental history of R&D candidates (R&D Focus 1999).

The qualitative analysis of outliers provided convincing evidences supporting the exclusion of the values from the model. Large scale, randomised studies are not ethically acceptable for treatment of cancer or HIV: the related candidates for R&D development receive an accelerated route to FDA submission, significantly faster than conventional medicines. In another case, the approval took much longer than expected due to the negative response of FDA of the initial submission. The model resisted the first methodological critique.

Reduced the variability inherent to secondary data, the average duration of the Pre-Clinical Phase was still much shorter in the model (2 years) than in the literature (5-7 years). A thorough discussion with scientists at SPRI (Schering Plough Research Institute) provided an acceptable explanation for the difference: pharmaceutical companies publish data on Toxicology studies only, which on average take one third of the total Pre-Clinical time.

The Author decided to de-construct the R&D timeline, applying a cost function to the Clinical Development Phases to discuss the implications of a basic sensitivity analysis.

The project was a fascinating opportunity to integrate different perspectives into a unique critical document. The cost function was formulated based on the inputs received in a brainstorming session with MIEM students (Master in Economics of Bocconi SDA Graduate School of Business – Milan). The Medline online database was chosen as a source for secondary data, obtaining 441 clinical papers related to a sample of 25 New Chemical Entities marketed in 1999.

Applying the cost function to the Patient Model, the Time-Cost Model of Clinical Pharmaceutical R&D was derived.

The following table, summarising the research outcomes, was presented at the *Accounting and Finance Colloquium*, held at the Henley Management College in July 2000.

Figure 2: Evidence based Time-Cost model of Pharmaceutical R&D

Time-Cost Model of Clinical Pharmaceutical R&D

Internal Medicine

	Pre-clin.	Phase 1	Phase 2	Phase 3	Pre-reg	Total
Time months	25+	13	25	25	9	**97+**
Cost $ million	n/a	2.5	13.0	(45.0)	1.5	**62.0**

Specialty

	Pre-clin.	Phase 1	Phase 2	Phase 3	Pre-reg	Total
Time months	25+	13	25	25	9	**97+**
Cost $ million	n/a	1.0	11.0	(24.5)	1.5	**38.0**

22

MODELLING RISK AND VALUE OF R&D PROJECTS.

Risk is a potential variation in outcomes: it is an objective measure (Williams 1995). Risk can also be defined as the measure of the probability and consequence of not achieving a defined project goal (Kerzner 1995). The second definition refers to project where the risk is not *symmetrical*: the risk of project failure is predominant than the risk of exceeding the expected value of the project.

In decision theory, risk is distinguished from uncertainty: *risk* refers to events that occur with a defined probability, while *uncertainty* of events cannot be quantified (Morgan & Henrion 1990).

The main elements of performing a risk analysis (Vose 1996) are:

➢ Definition of a suitable model

➢ Determination of probability distributions for the uncertain variables

➢ Consideration of interdependencies between the uncertain variables

➢ Analysis of the model

In development projects, there are two alternative ways to structure decision problems: influence diagrams and decision trees (Clemen 1991). An *influence diagram* is a rather simple graphical representation of a decision problem. Elements of the decision are the uncertainty events (circles), the decision to make (squares) and the value related to the event (rectangles with rounded corners). An Influence diagram reflects the decision situation at a certain time: it must include those decision elements that contribute to the immediate decision.

Figure 3: Influence diagram: of simultaneous evaluation of uncertain events.

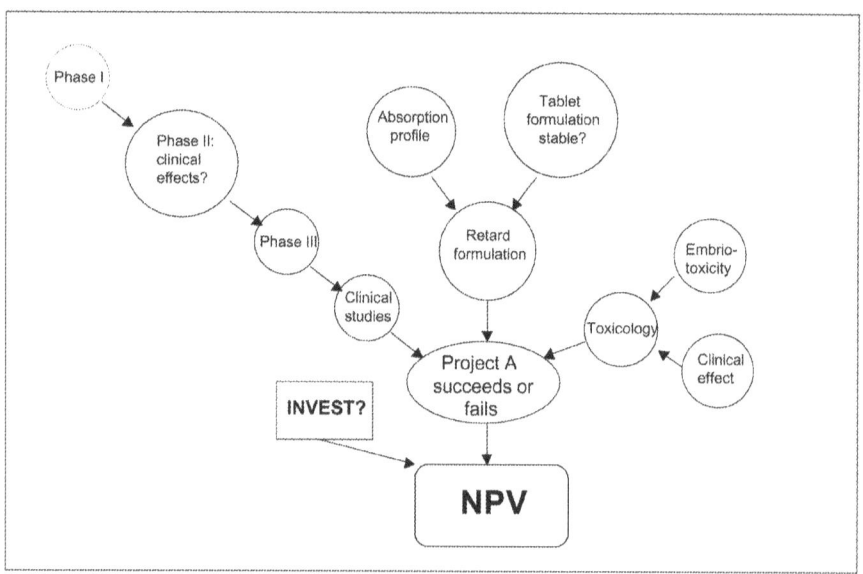

The major limits of influence diagrams are related to the insufficient clarity to chart complex decisions and to the impossibility to quantify risk.

Decision trees analysis is a useful tool to structure large and complex development projects (Shub 1994), as extensive projects can be represented as a series of chance nodes and their possible outcomes. To determine probabilities, outcomes must be *mutually exclusive* (only one outcome will occur) and *collectively exhaustive* (all possible outcomes are included).

Figure 4: Probability of the possible outcomes of an event.

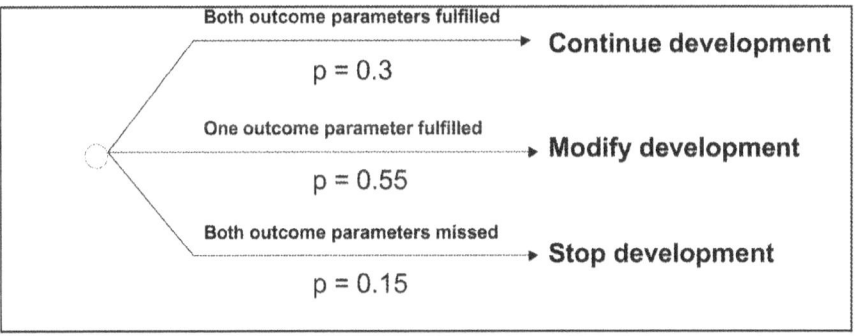

Development risks are defined as those directly related to the completion of the project plan up to the registration of the NCE (Cohen and Posner 1995).

When the development risks relevant to the project are identified, it is possible to design a model of the development risks, the project decision tree (Peace 1990).

Figure 5: Common risks related to Pharmaceutical R&D (Datamonitor, 1997)

Toxicology	Specifications for required dose range not fulfilled, carcinogenicity, embryotoxicity.
Clinical Pharmacology	Unfavourable bioavailability, unfavourable interaction with commonly used drugs, food interaction.
Clinical Development	Insufficient efficacy, comparison to clinical profile of competitors, add-on effects, safety problems, unfavourable effects in certain age groups or genetic phenotypes.
Chemistry	Preferred formulation not feasible or too expensive.
Chemical Development	Upscaling difficulties.
Costs	Development activities exceeding budget.
Schedule	Delays due to problems in delivering sufficient clinical trials material, priority conflict among development projects, difficult patient recruitment, modifications of clinical development plan.
Registration	Regulatory environment changes, absence of guidelines, different national requirements.
Marketing	Market penetration, competitive performance, physician's attitude, patients' compliance, and generics' market share erosion.

COST-BENEFIT ANALYSIS.

Until 1950s criteria used for research budgets were mostly subjective and R&D costing was primarily of an expense accounting nature. Then, starting in early 1950s, strategic planning began to call for maximising the present value of future streams of income. Both increasing taxation of profits and heightened competition in the post war period began to take their toll on corporate profits, a trend that increased into the early 1970s. Targets for returns on new risky efforts, such as R&D projects, rose accordingly. Reciprocal relationship between the cost of money and payback periods cut time horizons appreciably.

By the mid-1960s a consensus began to develop that the optimum budget level should be established judgementally between two extreme limits. Minimum is the level below which the effort would be ineffective and unstable because not enough research resources are available to provide mutual stimulation for a viable project. Maximum would be based on limits of financial and human resources in the company, including the effect of excessive R&D spending on current earnings. Toward the end of the 1960s, a bottom up strategy appeared. A "should be" budget level, assuming costs were not a problem, would be built up from the sum of suitable projects, patent position desired and needs of marketing and manufacturing.

By now enough quantified objective methods have been well defined that is surprising that companies arrive at their R&D budgets by either an analysis of their technological needs to support their business strategy, or an analysis of their competitors technological activities, or a mixture of both.

Because return on R&D investments is often difficult to calculate, the use of proxies, numbers that are related to R&D returns, can be demonstrated to be good approximations by statistical techniques (L. Ellis in *Managing Innovation for Profit*, Technical Insights Inc, 1987).

Undiscounted benefit-to-cost ratio is useful if R&D projects have similar time cycles and an appropriately larger ratio than the hurdle rate.

Cash flow payback is the number of years taken to recover the R&D investment from rewards, assuming that enough years of reward follow the payback period to earn an R&D return. This number tends toward the reciprocal of internal rate of return. Reciprocal of the hurdle discount rate become the maximum allowable payback time and only R&D projects that show shorter payback periods than this should be accepted.

Sales-to-development ratio relies on there being an average return on sales in the company with low standard deviation, so sales and profits are closely correlated. Benefit, as a proxy for

R&D return, is that for longer-range projects, sales may often be estimated long before it is possible to calculate R&D return.

Post evaluation of R&D financial results have long been advocated. Problem is knowing how much post-evaluation is productive: too much will begin to cut into effectiveness of R&D itself, lowering R&D return more than it raises it. Better project cost control systems would forecast R&D project costs, then accumulate control information in such a way that at any time actual costs with forecast could be compared.

Jerome T. Coe (in *Managing Innovation for Profit*, Technical Insights Inc, 1987) points out that the business output desired from R&D investment is the creation of new products, and more important, new products whose value to the customer will be reflected in new product sales in the years ahead. Consequently, analysts have to provide for a time-lagged evaluation, or an evaluation that will continue long enough to permit a judgement as to success of the R&D effort.

As the resources employed in R&D can be readily measured in terms of their costs, the input measure is the cost of R&D. This is typically defined as the R&D cost in a particular year. An index of R&D productivity is obtained by comparing the output, defined as the margins from new product sales, with the input (R&D cost). To derive the **productivity index**, Coe measures the product margins from the new product sales and compares the cumulative product margins with the cost of R&D.

Noting that product margin is the margin available to the business between the sales price and the cost of delivering that product to the customer, he defines product cost in this case as the direct manufacturing and marketing cost of delivering that product; he excludes the R&D component of that cost because the concept being developed is the liquidation of the R&D cost by the new product sales margins. He includes in the product cost a charge for depreciation, since expanding product lines frequently bring a necessary manufacturing output increase, which in turn must add a depreciation cost element as a consequence of growth.

Success can now be quantified by a productivity index that is conveniently expressed as **payback time**. Coe finds it useful to plot the sales growth of each of the annual product groups beginning with their year of introduction, and continuing with their sales in each of the following years.

Having analysed the product line sales in terms of annual product groups, it is possible to develop a quantitative productivity measurement for the R&D output by defining a payback time for it. Clearly, the faster the payback time or, in other words, the higher the return on that R&D investment, the more successful the R&D effort has been.

Coe acknowledges that in most R&D organisations the R&D effort of the current year cannot be precisely matched with that which is needed to produce the products which come out of the process in that year. Nevertheless if the payback time calculation is consistently applied year after year, this is not an impossible concept. Critical is to be consistent in relating the products of year n with the R&D cost of year n.

Another technique Coe finds useful for easy communication throughout an R&D organisation is to tally the new sales at the earliest possible moment – and consistently – so that trends can be observed and actions taken to make any necessary improvement. To do this, he recommends taking the shortest time period in the business, which gives a meaningful sales result (a quarter), and annualising the sales results at the 18-month point and again at the three-year point. This gives an early signal as to how valuable the previous year's R&D output of new products is going to be for the business, long term.

MANAGEMENT INFORMATION AND DECISION SCIENCES.

Sandoz Ltd, the Swiss pharmaceutical company merged with Ciba to create *Novartis*, has been assigning probabilities for technical success to all development projects since 1972. Forecasts are made by a panel of about a dozen R&D department heads as well as by some clinical specialists. Initially, each expert receives a list of all projects in development and assigns a probability for the technical success of each. In a second round, panellists receive the list of projects with the probabilities assigned by each of their colleagues. Following this – and unlike the usual Delphi exercise – the experts meet with the R&D Director to get to a consensus forecast for each project.

According to M. Menke (in *Managing Innovation for Profit*, Technical Insights Inc, 1987), this has the great advantage of allowing the group to consider aspects that really should have more weight than others. It also allows the R&D Director, who ultimately establishes the consensus forecast, to modify individual forecasts based on judgement of their validity and biases.

A typical schedule for this procedure at Sandoz takes two months, with each panel expert spending perhaps two to four hours on forecasting activity. Analysis of the results since 1972 reveals that " the individual project success probabilities accurately foretold the frequencies of ultimate success," Menke reports.

More and more senior management worries about returns on R&D investments. Placing a value on R&D is difficult because R&D decisions are characterised by uncertainty, long time horizons and a number of other dimensions that make them resistant to traditional financial evaluation methods.

Ciba-Geigy and Roche find that these evaluation difficulties can be counteracted, if not actually eliminated, through **decision analysis**.

Very briefly, this involves constructing influence diagrams and decision trees that illustrate the chronological sequence of decisions and uncertainties affecting a particular project. By providing a logical and consistent means of visualising uncertainty, complex problems, Menke considers decision trees ideal for describing to top management the real decision problems that are too difficult to solve logically.

Menle explains how decision analysis mitigates the factors that make R&D decision-making so difficult.

Uncertainty. After an influence diagram has identified the sources of uncertainty, sensitivity analysis ranks the importance of the various uncertainties, thus determining which ones are the most critical to the problem at hand. Once probability has been used to help people quantify their judgements about these most critical factors, a decision tree can be constructed in which the various branches represent different scenarios that combine the various technical and commercial possible outcomes. In essence, the entire structure of decision analysis is designed to deal with uncertainty.

Long time horizons. Rather than ignore speculations about the success of a project that will not be observable for years, different scenarios can be constructed that indicate the value of a project in different possible futures, corresponding to different degrees of technical and commercial success.

Poor communication between R&D and Marketing. The goal of decision analysis is to assign a value to the project. The underlying goal, according to Menke (1987) is to use that value to try the surface all the critical issues and thereby make the communication more open and effective.

Many alternatives. Lots of different R&D projects compete for limited resources, and any one project could be managed in many possible ways. Decision analysis provides a powerful way of determining the best developmental strategy for an individual project. The, at a higher level, it can be used for managing a portfolio of projects, weighing one against another to determine the optimum mix for the organisation.

Complex interactions. Projects are not independent of one another. Common aspects of R&D process can be shared among several projects, thus reducing costs; the commercial value of two or more jointly successful projects may be greater than the sum of their individual commercial values. The technical success of a new breakthrough product may make obsolete less sophisticated products under development. Information pertaining to the success or failure of one project may influence the assessment of technical success on other projects. Several parallel projects increase the likelihood that at least one will succeed technically; a successful R&D effort in the core area of business may increase the overall vulnerability of the Company.

The dynamic and sequential nature of R&D. With a decision tree, managers can examine, first, the decision on the various funding levels or directions of the applied research program and the different probabilities of achieving the desired result. This, in turn, leads to decisions about the kind of development program to undertake. Aim of the program is to deliver a product or process that can be commercialised at a particular time, cost and level of utility.

Difficult value issues. Decision analysis allows a company to take a broader view of its R&D effort by incorporating multiple factors, such as outsourcing, patent position or off licensing, into a decision tree.

Breakdown of risk criteria. Decision analysis is a way of dealing with many of the characteristics of R&D that make it so difficult to evaluate by traditional financial analysis.

Determining the productivity of R&D based organisations is difficult because their output is largely intangible and cannot be measured objectively. However a technique known as **output mapping** deals explicitly with subjective assessments, and in such a way that R&D managers can interpret the information in a manner useful for decision making.

According to M.B. Packer (in *Managing Innovation for Profit*, Technical Insights Inc, 1987), the key steps in the output mapping are:

- ☐ Identify the intended use of the productivity information.
- ☐ Identify the goals and objectives of the organisation.
- ☐ Identify those activities performed by members of the organisation that involve transferring of information.
- ☐ Identify the resources devoted to these activities.

- ☐ Identify specific indicators that measure the extent or level of each activity or resource identified in the preceding steps.

- ☐ Perform a factor analysis on the data collected.

- ☐ Ask managers to rank order projects using their intuitive sense of overall output.

- ☐ Perform a factor analysis of the subjective scores.

- ☐ Explain the results of the analysis.

- ☐ Examine the output maps from a strategic perspective.

One characteristic of output mapping is that management can experiment analytically with new resource allocations or strategies. If a shift in R&D emphasis is suggested, management can estimate the change this shift will cause in the subjective assessments using the original indicators. Projected positions on the output maps can be then computed from these estimated values in the same manner that the factor scores were computed previously from the original assessments. This gives management a tool that is flexible and easy to interpret for planning at the same time as it integrates the intangible aspects of R&D activities and output with the more traditional tangible measures.

Forecasting methods to project R&D contribution to sales have been used by Merck Sharp & Dohme Laboratories since 1972.

Basically Merck examines each of more 100 projects in its R&D portfolio for three characteristics:

☐ The probability of success inherent to each project.

☐ The market potential if the project succeeds.

☐ Time to market: when the new product will reach the market.

Then a Monte Carlo computer simulation provides an estimate of the value of the entire portfolio, together with the rate at which contributions to sales will occur. It also provides an estimate of the uncertainty associated with the sales in any given year (V.J. Pecore in *Managing Innovation for Profit*, Technical Insights Inc, 1987).

An allowance fore uncertainty has been built into each project assessment, so there is no need to guess at the uncertainty for the total program. Since the input is obtained on a project-by-project basis, excessively high estimates can be assumed to cancel excessively low estimates. Even errors in revenue estimates of up to 25% will not grossly change the conclusions because the output is obtained in ranges.

The concept of **Zero-Base Budgeting (ZBB)** is critical for R&D managers when their funding is completely discretionary.

They need to justify the resources needed and to make sure that research funding is allocated to the potentially most profitable projects.

ZBB forces this kind of justification by requiring managers to evaluate each project in its entirety, identifying alternatives and justifying conclusions, rather than simply assuming last year's level of expenditures.

P.A. Pyhrr (in *Managing Innovation for Profit*, Technical Insights Inc, 1987) stresses that because ZBB reveals explicitly what will or will not happen to specific projects for various level of funding, top management is thereby forced to make conscious tradeoffs between research and operational expenditures rather than just "cut research by 10%" as it often finds so easy to do under budget pressures.

Zeneca and the Manchester Business School reported an analytical hierarchy process for evaluation of R&D project (Isley quoted by Warr 1998).

The structural hierarchy used had eight attributes and assessments were obtained using AHP software. The attributes were:

> technical feasibility (biological, clinical and chemical)

> therapeutic need

- ➢ competitive position

- ➢ general support

- ➢ ancillary uses

- ➢ competence of staff

- ➢ research investment

- ➢ product champion

Research-based companies are highly dependent on certain highly innovative individuals whom Cox (1989) refers to as "product champions". Some key attributes of a product champion are scientific ability, experience, communicating skills, leadership, flexibility, perseverance and decisiveness. (Isley *at al.* 1991)

The eight attributes in the model were weighted by project managers, who differed considerably in their score for therapeutic need and competence of staff. The AHP technique proved not to be ideal, in that it judged on pairwise comparisons. New software, Judgmental Analysis System (JAS), was developed at Manchester Business School. Detailed word models were established as standard reference frames with anchor points made explicit.

The whole system has reportedly been developed into a simple judgmental model that has been used for a number of years.

At the beginning of last decade, Bayer pioneered the concept of a *standard project*; a benchmark derived from known data on the probability of success of R&D projects, with which to compare other projects (McNeil 1996).

Bayer's standard project used six pre-clinical hurdles and eight clinical ones. The usual Phase I, II, and III milestones were not used. Instead, hurdles such as effectiveness, formulation and competition were taken into account. Compared to standard project, a high-medium-low feasibility estimate was derived. For example, feasibility might be high where the project scored five times as highly than the standard project in the same development stage.

Feasibility scores were then combined with maximum sales potential to provide an estimate of maximum NPV. If the cost of resources equalled maximum NPV, the project was abandoned early in the development process. The same research team developing the project made decisions, because they were able to understand the qualitative nature of data evaluated. The standard project approach was intended to reduce serendipity, but the evaluation was still dependent on a number of soft factors of importance, including R&D strategy, desire for innovation and blockbuster obsession.

In terms of qualifying risks for highly innovative compounds, a methodology has been developed by Double Helix Development, which assesses and scores a number of factors:

- ☐ Market size
- ☐ Unmet medical needs
- ☐ Satisfaction with current treatment
- ☐ Potential clinical benefit
- ☐ Technical and regulatory feasibility
- ☐ Potential competition
- ☐ Time to market

This enables a quantitative score to be derived for a product that then leads to a commercial value estimate. There is a balance between what is rational, derived from expert views and internal company knowledge and that from experience, which most project leaders will successfully draw upon. However, for a novel product in a novel indication, a correct balance between the two is critical and an external expert opinion should always be considered when the company has no prior expertise in the therapeutic area.

PARAMETRIC COST MODELS
TO ESTIMATE RESEARCH COST.

The application of Parametric Cost Analysis to pharmaceutical development can help estimate the cost of Phase III trials, the most investment-intensive stage of research.

Wooding (1994) identified four noncost variables driving sample size and therefore cost of pharmaceutical research in humans: critical difference, risk of failing to detect a difference greater than delta, the risk of falsely claiming that a difference exists, the estimated expected experimental error.

The Phase III Clinical Experimental Design Function can be derived as a mathematical equation, accurately estimating the number of patients (proxy of cost) required to prove (or disprove) the chosen clinical outcome.

The derived Cost Estimating Relationship (CER) of Phase III Clinical Trials resulted as a useful tool to reduce the uncertainty related to cost estimates: more complex Parametric Cost Models could be used to model the entire Pharmaceutical R&D process, from discovery to development.

Parametric cost analysis uses equations to map measurable system attributes into cost (Dean 1989). The measures of the system attributes are called metrics. The equations are called cost estimating relationships (CER), and are obtained by the analysis of cost and technical metric data of products analogous to those to be estimated. Johnston (1960) provides foundational theory, methods and results on case studies.

Klein and Tait (1971), an early example of applied parametric cost analysis, expresses the number of tool design and tool fabrication hours per part in terms of the number of drilled and reamed holes, the volume of the piece, the number of locating points, and the complexity of part orientation. Stepwise regression was used to select these statistically significant variables for a linear equation from the eleven chosen as possible cost drivers. The authors also introduce the reality of cost uncertainty through a trade off of confidence and expected time.

Today, parametric estimating is usually applied to large systems, such as those found in the U.S. Department of Defence or NASA. Thus, parametric estimating relies on simulation models that are system of statistically and logically supported mathematical equations. The impacts of a product's physical, performance and programmatic attribute on cost and schedule are defined by these equations. Tailoring parameters are used to describe the object being estimated. Output of the model is validated with data from past projects. The object to be estimated is described by choosing specific values for the independent variables in the equation that represents the characteristics of the object. The equations are then used to extrapolate from past and current experience to forecast the cost of future products.

The basic assumption is that a measurable relationship exists between system attributes and the cost of the system: if a function exists, the attributes are cost drivers.

Sample size variables are constraints on the Clinical Development Process (Wooding 1994). From optimisation theory we know that any active constraint generates cost by not permitting full optimisation of the objective. Thus, sample size variables are cost drivers

The typical statistical process (Draper and Smith 1981) is to find a value for m parameters $p = (p_1 ... p_k)$ such that the cost y can be predicted reasonably well by the equation $y = f(x, p) + e$ where e is the prediction error and $x = (x_1 ... x_m)$ is a set of measures of system characteristics that vary over n cases $(y_i x_{1i} ... x_{mi})$, different for each $i = 1, n$.

The above equation is the general form for response surface methodology (Box and Draper 1987).

Thus, from a statistical perspective, parametric cost analysis may be viewed as an application of response surface methodology to the field of cost analysis (Dean 1992).

CER is a mathematical expression relating cost as the dependent variable to one or more independent cost-driving variables.

The continuum of CERs is synonymous with the term parametric estimating methods. Parametric estimating methods are defined as estimating techniques that rely on theoretical, known or proven relationships between item characteristics and the associated item cost. Whether labelled a CER or a parametric estimating method, the technique relies on a value, called a parameter, to estimate the value of something else, typically cost. The estimating relationship can range in complexity from something rather simple; such as a numerical expression of value or a ratio (typically expressed as a percentage), to something more complex; such as a multi-variable mathematical expression.

The key notion is that the cost of one element is used to estimate, or predict, the cost of another element. When the relationship is described as a cost-to-noncost relationship, the reference is to a CER where a *characteristic* of an item is used to predict the item's *cost*.

For CERs to be valid, they must be developed using sound logical concepts. The logic concept is one where experts in the field agree, as supported by generally accepted theory, that one of the variables in the relationship (the independent variable) causes or affects the behaviour in another variable (the dependent variable). Once valid CERs have been developed, parametric cost modelling and estimating can proceed.

Figure 6: CER Development Process

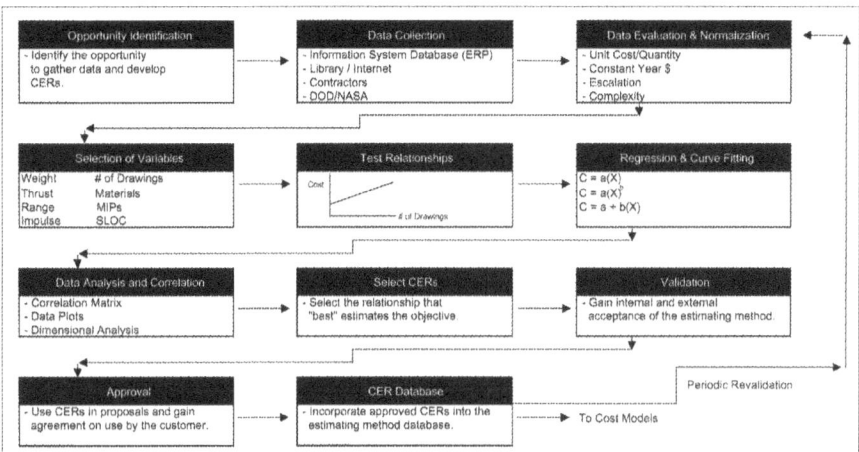

CRITICAL STEPS:

1. *Parameters identification*: a fundamental requirement for the inclusion of noncost variable in a CER would be that is a significant predictor of cost. As discussed before, the number of patients enrolled is the primary cost driver of Phase 3 Clinical Trials. Wooding (1994) the required Clinical Trials sample size as a function of four parameters (noncost variables): critical difference, risk of failing to detect a difference greater than delta, the risk of falsely claiming that a difference exists, the estimated expected experimental error.

2. *Data collection*: primary data are reported in the statistical section (sample sizing) of any clinical protocol.

3. *Data Normalisation:* estimating the expected experimental error (Wooding 1994). This step involves obtaining an estimate of the standard deviation of the selected measurement. Standard deviation values are always reported in the "Methodology" paragraph of Clinical Trial Papers. It must either be estimated by means of a pilot trial (small-scale pivotal trial) or obtained from one or more previous set of data, derived from a previous study similar in all respects to the projected trial. The normalised parameter is equal to delta in terms of the number of estimated sigmas. It is calculated by dividing the specified delta value by the estimated value of sigma.

5. ***Derive the CER model using Multiple Regression***: In simple regression analysis, a single independent variable (X) is used to estimate the dependent variable (Y), and the relationship is assumed to be linear (a straight line). This is the most common form of regression analysis used in CER development. However, there are more complex versions of the regression equation that can be used that consider the effects of more than one independent variable. Multiple regression analysis, for example, assumes that the change in Y can be better explained by using more than one independent variable.

$$Y_c = a + b_1 X_1 + b_2 X_2$$

where:

Y_c = the calculated or estimated value for the dependent variable

a   = the Y intercept, the value of Y when all X-variables = 0

X_1 = the first independent (explanatory) variable

b1   = the slope of the line related to the change in X1: the value by

which Yc changes when X1 changes by one

X_2 = the second independent variable

b2   = the slope of the line related to the change in X2: the value by

which Y_c changes when X_2 changes by one

Step-wise regression is the process of "introducing the X variables one at a time (stepwise forward regression) or by including all the possible X variables in one multiple regression and rejecting them one at a time (stepwise backward regression). The decision to add or drop a variable is usually made on the basis of the contribution of that variable to the ESS [error sum of squares], as judged by the *F*- test." Stepwise regression allows the analyst to add variables, or remove them, in search of the best model to predict cost.

There is no one statistic that disqualifies a CER or model, nor is there any one statistic that "validates" a CER or model. The math modelling effort must be examined from a complete perspective, starting with the data and logic of the relationship.

Only after ensuring that the data and the logic of the relationship are solid should the analyst begin evaluating the statistical quality of the model. Statistical examination includes an evaluation of the individual variables in the model. The t-stat for each explanatory variable is the most common method to evaluate the variable's significance in the relationship. The next step is to assess the significance of the entire equation. The F-stat is the most common statistic used to assess this quality of the entire equation. Assuming the individual variable(s) and the entire equation have significance, the next step is to judge the size and proportion of the equation's estimating error. The standard error of the estimate (SEE or SE) and coefficient of variation (CV) provide this insight.

Finally, the typical statistical analysis concludes with examining the value of the coefficient of determination (R^2), or Adjusted R^2 when comparing models with a different number of independent variables for each model.

The coefficient of determination measures the percentage of the variation in the dependent variable explained by the independent variable(s).

Finally, a critical piece of any evaluation is to identify the range of the independent values on which the model was built. Theoretically, the model is only valid over this relevant range of the independent value data. In practice, use of the model is permissible outside of this range so long as the hypothesised mathematical relationship remains valid. This is likely to be only a small limit beyond the actual values of the data. The range of validity is a judgement call and should rely on those knowledgeable in the element being estimated to help establish over what range the CER will provide reasonable predictions.

FINANCIAL AND RISK ANALYSIS MODELS

A number of models have been designed combining financial project evaluation with probabilistic risk analysis .Yet, SDG has found that in many successful research-based Pharmaceutical companies, 10-15% of the R&D budget is spent on "white elephant" projects: those that are technically difficult and will not be a commercial success even if technical hurdles are surmounted (Matheson and Matheson 1995)

One simple way of comparing projects is a "bubble chart" in which NPV is plotted against probability of regulatory approval, but the "points" in the plot are in fact "bubbles", the diameters of which are related to project cost (Arnold 1995).

More complex are multi-attribute models which take more factors into account (e.g., medical benefit, potential market size) in a risk analysis using programs such as @Risk or LSE Equity (Phillips 1995).

An "experts" forum may be added to identify strategy options for each project, in which case Phillips refers to the model as a "socio-economic" one, based on the personalistic view of probability. From the personalistic perspective, the probability of an event is the degree of belief that a person has that this event will occur. The person takes into account all relevant information that he/she is currently aware of (Morgan and Henrion 1990).

An advantage of the socio-economic approach is that it may also help to improve communication within the company.

Making decisions about relative priorities between projects is based on the examination of a range of criteria. Typically they will include the potential commercial value of the research outcome, the probability of the project's success, the total cost of completing the project and bringing the product to market and the time to market (Baker 1998).

Taylor (1997) lists research opportunities, medical need, patient potential, product convenience, cost of goods, competition, R&D capabilities and portfolio balance.

In screen set-up or early phases, technical feasibility is a major concern. Factors to be assessed include screen type, molecular target, selectivity, in vitro function testing, in vivo models, chemical opportunity and proof of principle, e.g. ensuring that the molecular target does relate to the indication pursued by clinical trials (Bogner and Thomas 1996)

Over the last decade, the approach to strategic management of Drug Development has been progressively rationalised, in parallel to the development of financial and risk analysis quantitative models.

To describe the evolution of R&D projects valuation, the Author will briefly discuss just the few exemplary models whose methodology and outcomes have been published.

A recent survey (Bode Greuel 1996) performed on European pharmaceutical companies revealed that 72% of the 36 participants consider correct financial project evaluation as absolutely critical for research project decisions.

Large differences, however, exist with regards to the evaluation models applied. Only 53% use the NPV technique; in particular, smaller firms (< 500 employees) do not apply the NPV algorithm.

These results confirm the findings of the Centre for Medicine Research International, who found that 55% of the surveyed pharmaceutical companies were dissatisfied with the evaluation model they applied (McFarlane and Walker 1995).

The payback period rule is still used in 67% of the surveyed companies, in 22% as the only method applied, and in 45% in combination with NPV or IRR.

The payback period is found by counting the number of years it takes for the cumulated forecasted cash flows to equal the initial investment.

The IRR (Internal Rate of Return) represents the rate at which the discounted cash inflows equal the discounted cash outflows NPV = 0 (Brealey Myers 1996). The payback period calculation ignores any cash inflows beyond the payback period. Furthermore, the time-value of money is not generally taken into account.

IRR is intrinsic to the project, showing its limits in multi-period projects where the subsequent cash flows exhibit changes of sign.

IRR also ignores the issue of scale (large returns on small investment compared to small returns on large investments).

In conclusion, the application of payback period and IRR may produce inaccurate judgements, leading to sub-optimal investment decisions (Mills 1994).

INTEGRATION OF NPV AND RISK ANALYSIS.

Bode-Greuel (1997) has developed a rational approach to financial project evaluation.

NPV and risk analysis are combined in a unique model that has been developed to determine the expected project NPV.

The application of the NPV algorithm implies that future cash flows have to be discounted to their present value. The discount rate should appropriately reflect the capital market risk of the pharmaceutical business. The discount rate is calculated according to the *capital asset pricing model* (CAPM). If the capital structure of a company consist of equity and debt, the tax advantage and smaller cost of debt is taken into account by calculating the *weighted average cost of capital* (r_{WACC}). Pharmaceutical companies operate in all major markets and have investors that live in various countries. The expected return on equity is considered from the perspective of a shareholder who holds an internationally diversified portfolio of pharmaceutical stocks in order to reduce risk

Based on Investor's return on equity, r_{WACC} is considered from the perspective of a specific company ant its capital structure. All forecasted cash flows are considered from the next upcoming investment until the end of the product life cycle. Sunk and overhead costs are not included in Bode-Greuel model. The terminal value of a project is the remaining net cash flows after patent expiration calculated as perpetuity. Since the discount rate only reflects capital market risks, other risks related to the investment, such as development or sales risks, are addressed by an appropriate probabilistic analysis of expected cash flows.

The expected project NPV is defined as the probability-weighted sum of the scenario NPVs (Bode Greuel 1997). It is a single number representing the financial value of the project corrected by its risk.

Statistical processes can be applied in estimating development risks. "Go/no go" decisions at nodal points draw a project decision tree resulting in several development scenarios. The probability of each outcome is defined based on expert judgement.

Commercial risks affect anticipated market shares and sales forecasts. Extrapolation of past performances is preferred for short-term perspective. Judgmental model building approaches are used for long-range scenarios.

The expected project NPV is the central parameter for decision-making: if the value is positive, the project is worth investing.

When the expected project NPV turns out to be negative, a detailed value driver analysis should be completed. If there is no possibility to add value to a negative expected NPV outcome, the project is best dropped.

Based on the result of the model, the expected NPV can be plotted as frequency histogram visualising the project risk.

Figure 7: Expected NPV distribution as indication for project risk.

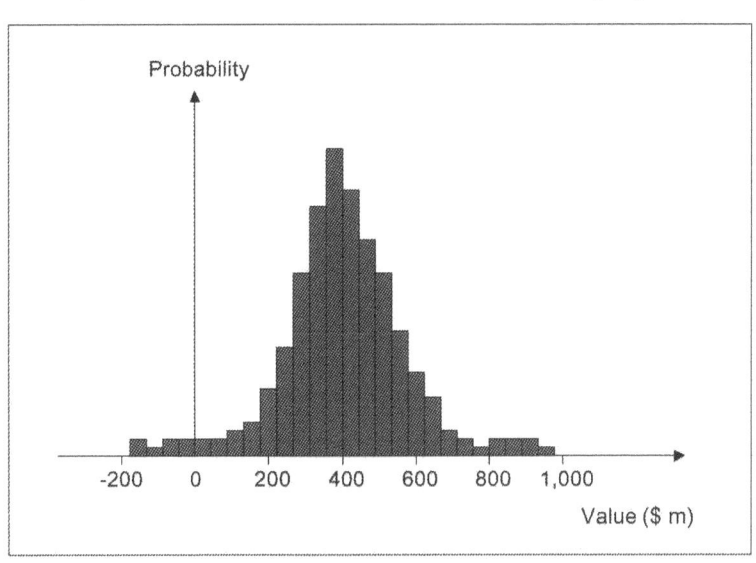

This decision support tool has several advantages over more basic financial models (*see payback period and IRR*): the expected NPV considers all cash flows generated over the product life cycle and it can model complex, multi-period projects where net cash flows may exhibit repeated changes of sign. The project value still critically depends on the judgmental assessment of project risks.

A basic sensitivity analysis reveals the limits of the model.

Assuming constant project costs, the following general statement can be made:

1. If the probability of development success is high, the expected project NPV is relatively high.

2. The higher the probability of optimistic scenarios, the higher is the expected NPV.

3. The higher the probability of scenarios assuming late project failure, the lower is the expected NPV.

4. The later in the project expensive clinical studies are scheduled, the higher is the expected NPV.

5. The earlier critical nodes are scheduled, the higher is the expected NPV.

5. The more critical nodes have to be completed, the lower is the expected NPV.

EVA®: DRIVER OF MARKET VALUE.

The term EVA was coined (and trademarked) by Stern Stewart & Co., a US consulting firm. EVA attempts to measure how much value was created by an organisation during an accounting period for its shareholders.

EVA is calculated by subtracting a capital charge from net operating profit after tax (NOPAT). NOPAT is a measure of after-tax operating profit, a common starting point in analysts' valuation models. NOPAT can also be viewed as a measure of unlevered profit, which is the profit a company would report if it were an all-equity firm (no debt in its capital structure). Financing costs are reflected in the weighted average cost of capital (WACC). The WACC is multiplied by investing capital, alternatively known as capital employed, to estimate the capital charges. These charges are then subtracted from NOPAT to derive EVA. Invested capital can be defined as total assets, net of non-interest bearing current liabilities.

In its unadjusted form, EVA is essentially the same as residual income, which is normally expressed as net income minus a charge for the cost of equity capital (with the cost of debt already reflected in net income).

Adjustments are required to achieve higher correlation between the short-term profit measure (in this case EVA) and share prices (Chen and Dodd 1997). These adjustments aim to:

1. Produce an EVA figure that is closer to cash flows and therefore less subject to the distortions of accrual accounting;

2. Remove the arbitrary distinction between investments in tangible assets, which are capitalised, and intangible assets, which tend to be written off as incurred;

3. Prevent the amortisation or write-off of goodwill;

4. Eliminate the use of successful efforts accounting;

5. Bring off-balance sheet debt into balance sheet;

6. Correct biases caused by accounting depreciation.

Eli Lilly's strategic intent is to be the global leader in targeted therapeutic areas, creating value via pharmaceutical innovation and capital management (McNeil 1996).

Primarily global market share and EVA$^{®}$ measure leadership

by explicitly considering the total cost of capital and adjusting the equity equivalent reserves, EVA$^{®}$ purportedly measures economic profits. EVA$^{®}$ allows investors to evaluate weather the return being earned on invested capital exceeds its cost as measured by the returns from alternative capital uses. Management may do different things to create value for the business.

The EVA® or value of a company increases (Chen & Dodd 1997) if it:

➢ raises operating profits without requiring excess capital

➢ uses less capital for the same level of operation

➢ invests in projects that earn more than the cost of capital

In order to better understand the drivers of EVA®, Lilly benchmarked a number of pharmaceutical companies, and conducted modelling of their expected project and portfolio data. From a sensitivity analysis of a number of variables, Lilly determined that two primary drivers of EVA® are price per Day of Therapy (innovation) and dose per DOT (a proxy for manufacturing capital employed).

Figure 8: Drivers of project to project EVA® variability.

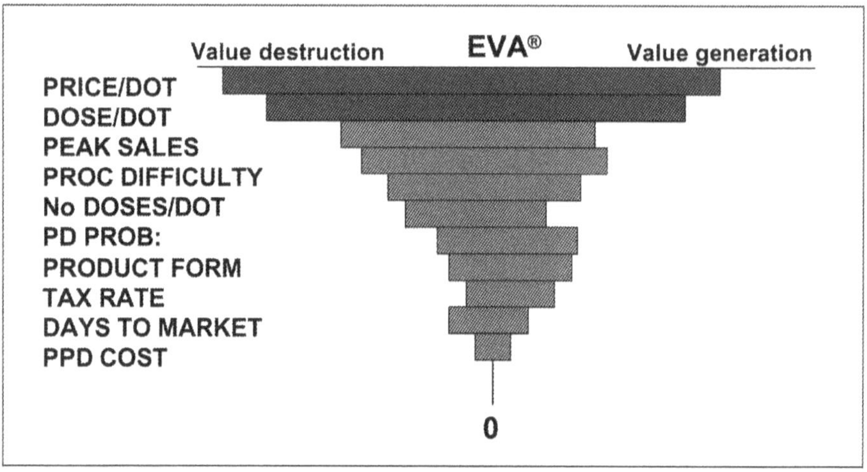

This analysis does not suggests that other factors (market size, sales, cost to develop) are not important, only that given the range of variability of factors, dose and price are critical considerations in understanding the value of an R&D project.

This analysis further supports the value of innovation to the extent that it impacts the price of a product (as well as the market share). In addition, the analysis suggests that the potency of a drug should be a key criterion when selecting value added R&D projects.

Following this lead, Lilly evaluates and prioritises R&D development projects according to the major drivers of EVA® creation:

➢ degree of innovation (expected price/DOT)

➢ potency (dose/DOT)

➢ expected peak sales

➢ global prevalence of the disease

Like the majority of financial performance measures, though, EVA® is inherently backward looking as it looks at the value added in a past accounting period and thus measuring the success of past strategic decisions and investments (Brabazon and Sweney 1998).

It fails to explicitly consider the current strategy being pursued by the organisation or by its major competitors and does not attempt to assess whether the organisation is taking actions to ensure it will develop and maintain a sustainable competitive advantage.

Commonly to NPV, EVA does not capture the value generated by interactions among projects, such as cash flow enhancement, synergies, risk accumulation, image effects and experience (Bode Greuel 1997).

EVA has also attracted considerable attention as an alternative to traditional accounting earnings for use in incentive compensation. EVA application guidelines at Eli Lilly are the following:

- ☐ Eli Lilly is among a pioneering group of companies that are tying pay to EVA goals.

- ☐ Eli Lilly started using out EVA around the middle of 1994.

- ☐ EVA causes to focus on capital expenditures.

- ☐ A cross-functional team discovered a shortcoming of the incentive system produced because the executive pay was linked to sales and net income.

- ☐ Eli Lilly developed a pay plan, tailored to its needs, with consultant Stern Stewart

- ☐ Lilly's bonus plan requires managers to achieve continuous, year-to-year EVA improvements.

- ☐ Lilly set EVA targets based on competitive factors.

- ☐ It raise the targets a small percentage every year to keep raising shareholder value.

- ☐ There is a bonus based on a proprietary formula if the targets are met.

- ☐ Decisions are made in alignment with EVA.

- ☐ Elli Lilly sees at EVA as a sophisticated financial tool that changes behaviour

- ☐ Linking bonuses to EVA is meant to change the whole culture.

- For the initial go-round, beginning in 1995, Lilly tied EVA to bonuses for the 90 most senior executives at Lilly.

- The plan is extending to a broader group each year to reach 1,400 executives in 1997.

- Successful EVA firms, have not made massive shifts to EVA all at once.

- Top-Bottom implemented.

- Work out the bugs and education of people is important.

- EVA drove a rapid change in attitudes toward capital throughout the business.

- Lilly analysed pros and cons in different firms that have approached EVA.

- It chose to base bonuses on corporate wide EVA performance.

- Lilly is able to carry the calculation down to the various business units for strategic purposes.

- Eli Lilly implemented global business units for the first time while implementing EVA too.

- Tying compensation to EVA Lilly got each individual business unit behaving in an optimum way.

- There is a danger that managers will make shortsighted investment decisions to boost their bonuses.

- ☐ To avoid that, Lilly set up a bonus bank that encourages managers to take a longer-term perspective.

- ☐ The bank acts as a long-term scorekeeper.

- ☐ Managers are accountable for the long-term effect of their decisions.

- ☐ There is theoretically no ceiling to the EVA bonus.

- ☐ All incentive plans are completely consistent with EVA

- ☐ Keep it as simple as you possibly

- ☐ People is doing slightly better with the EVA compensation system.

REAL OPTIONS

Options associated with value based project management are defined as *operating options*. Several types of operating options can be differentiated:

> ➢ Option *to defer*: the right to postpone an investment in order to benefit from resolution of uncertainty.

> ➢ Option *to abandon*: right to cancel future investments when interim results do not meet expectations.

> ➢ Option *to switch*: selectively invest in different applications.

> ➢ Option *to adapt operating scale*: operations may be expanded, contracted or temporarily shut down.

> ➢ Option *to improve*: opportunity to take corrective actions during the course of an R&D project.

Strategic or growth options are future opportunities to invest in activities not included in the initial project. Strategic options form the basis of innovation and support competitiveness, but there is often a tendency to neglect their value because difficult to assess.

Example: Pharmaceutical R&D

A drug company needed to value a new drug research and development project. There were four development phases:

□ Initial R&D with 20% chance of success

□ Preclinical testing, with 50% chance of success

□ Testing I, with 40% chance of success

□ Testing II, with a 90% chance of success.

Figure 9: Abandon Options in Pharmaceutical R&D

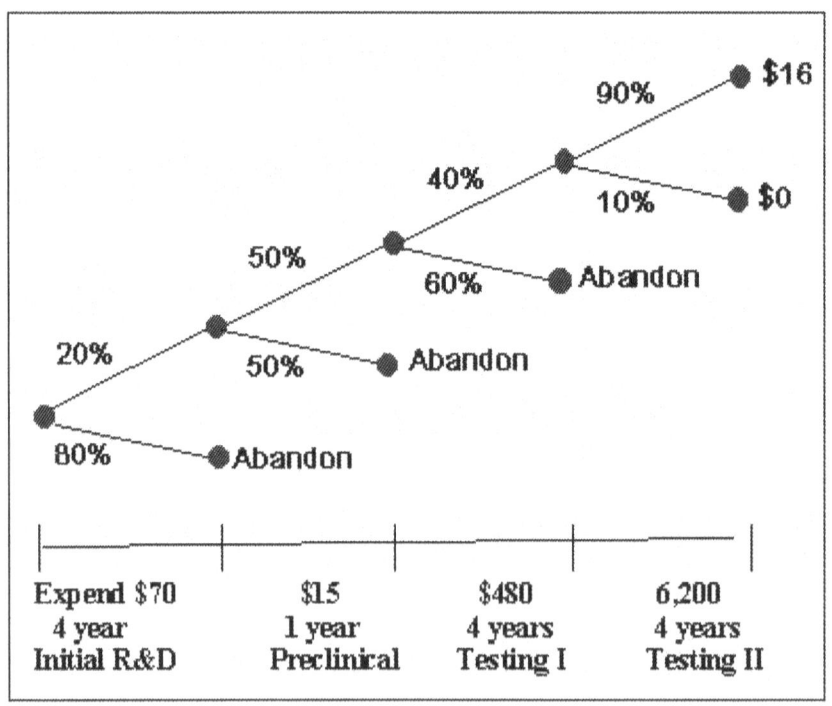

Several Real Options application to the pharmaceutical industry can be found in the literature. Some examples are:

- ☐ How valuable is the first stage of a multi-year drug development program?

- ☐ How can customer information be valued in an acquisition?

- ☐ What should the company pay for the rights to a technology when the commercial success of the pharmaceutical is highly uncertain?

- ☐ How much can the company spend to accelerate the development of a new product to insure it is first to market?

It is important to note that the decision (option) to invest in each development stage is based not on immediate returns but on achieving an ultimate, but risky, outcome. In traditional applications of options, stage-wise investment opportunities are called compound options. Valuation of the development program requires scenario formulation for a number of outcomes.

These outcomes are influenced by one or more uncertainties in pharmaceutical development, such as R&D success, efficacy and side effects, market demand, development timing and cost, price, and competitive products.

Figure 10: Value of options in Pharmaceutical R&D

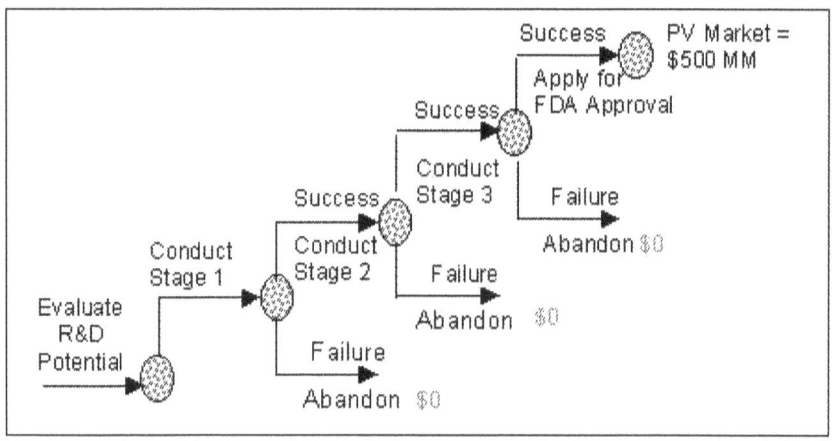

The Value of Research has many facets. Research creates a non-monetary value arising from the knowledge gained. Applied to basic Research in medicine, any discovery that increases the knowledge of the human organism may lead to better treatment of diseases. It is difficult, however, to assign a financial value to knowledge.

The pharmaceutical industry mostly pursues "applied research" expected to result in a marketable product in the future. Investments in platform technologies belong to this category, as they are undertaken to improve company's competitive position. As soon as decisions are pending with respect to selection and prioritisation of such projects, financial models in research should capture the strategic value of these investment options.

Merck-Sharp & Dohme is looking at Real Options to capture the financial value of R&D portfolio more accurately (Nichols 1994).

R&D projects are characterised by contingent decisions that depend on future outcomes. Conceptually, investing in the next R&D milestone can be considered as an investing in a call option on the forthcoming step and eventually on the final outcome. Out-licensing R&D candidates can be conversely considered as a put option. The value of managerial flexibility and upside potential of risk are not properly captured by traditional NPV: while higher risk translates into higher discount rates in traditional discounted cashflow models, real options evaluation rewards accepting risk by valuing the upside potential properly.

Merck identified two ways of applying real options in R&D project evaluation.

1. *Real options as a complement to NPV (**binomial method**)*. NPV is applied in a dynamic way, taking into account that R&D process is organised along milestones at which management will decide whether to abandon or continue with the project. The possible outcomes are displayed in decision trees. Risk is represented in probability estimates derived from average industry attrition rates.

Figure 11: Decision tree.

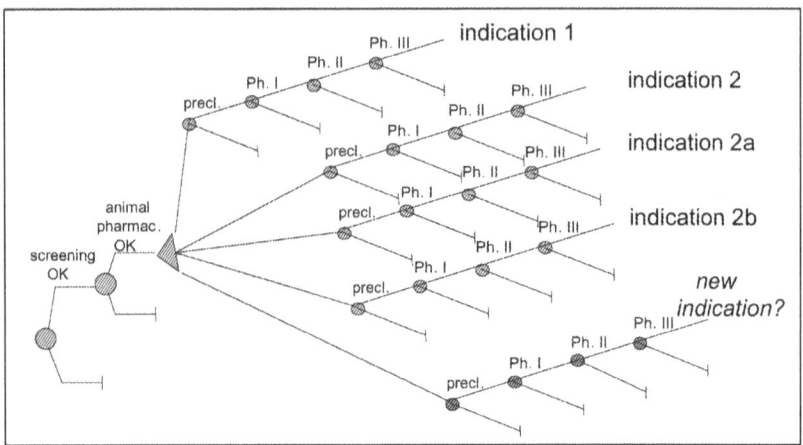

2. *Real options evaluation as a substitute to NPV*: applying financial option pricing methods to evaluate projects. Risk is represented in the assumed spread of asset value (binomial option pricing) or in a volatility parameter (Black and Scholes 1973). Financial option pricing can be applied when a marketed "twin" asset can be identified that has a similar risk profile as the asset to be evaluated, or when the underlying asset is a marketed product (i.e. development of new indications).

Figure 12: Investment opportunities using Option Pricing (Luehrman 1998)

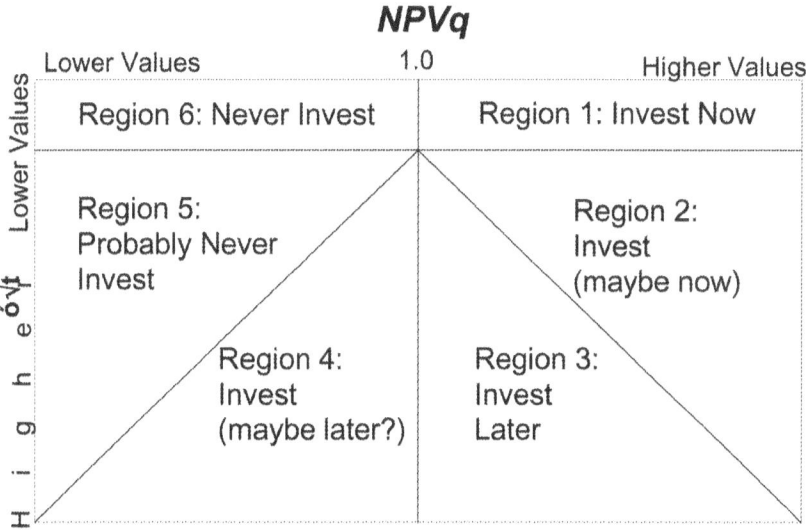

The Black-Scholes model is appealing because it simplifies the evaluation by using only five inputs: PV of project (S), development cost (X), time the project may be deferred (t), risk-free rate of return (rf) and development risk.

This model, though, obscures endogenous (technical) risk which play a critical role in R&D. The algorithm assumes that the value of underlying asset follows a symmetrical random walk with a linearly variance over time. Real Option pricing probably does not reflect the risk of a project where process and methodology may in itself be a matter of research.

Kerstin Bode-Greuel (1997 proposes an interesting approach to Real Options for the evaluation of research projects.

Figure 13: Suggested financial models (Bode Greuel 2000)

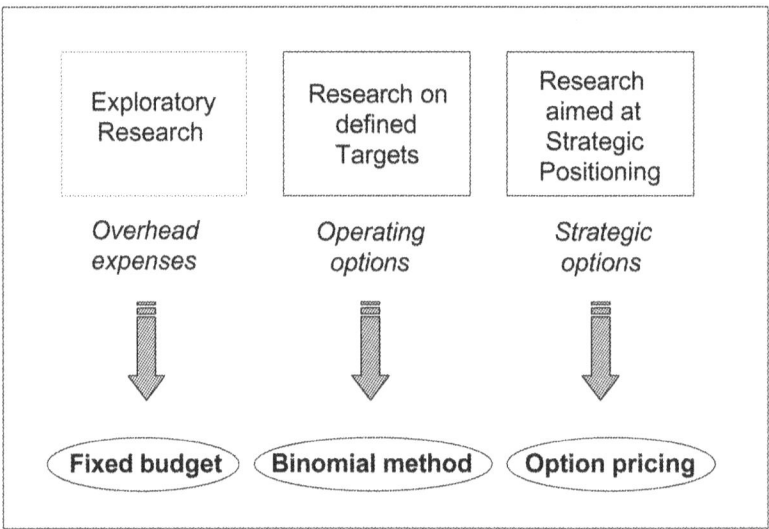

Conclusions and Future Research

Over the last twenty years, the evaluation of pharmaceutical R&D projects has been progressively moving away from deterministic quantitative analysis, in favour of non-linear, stochastic algorithms valuing the uncertainty of the research process.

Decision-making tools should satisfy four key requirements (Copeland & Keenan 1998):

- ➢ *Cashflow based*

- ➢ *Risk adjusted*

- ➢ *Multi-period*

- ➢ *Capture flexibility*

The greatest benefits from prolific discovery will go to organisation with superior capabilities in portfolio selection and progression (BCG 1999).

With enormous development costs per compound, and with candidates becoming much more abundant, pharmaceutical companies will need to develop sophisticated techniques, such as option pricing, to help them determine which compounds to advance at each stage.

Although most companies currently employ modelling tools to support development decisions, those tools are rarely used in the discovery process.

New discovery technologies are leading to pipelines not constrained by a limited number of promising compounds. At every level, from technology to leads to development, selection approaches become critical. This will demand better information management and a new emphasis on integration across disciplines.

Figure 14: Decision-Making tools (Rahmani 1999).

	Cashflow based	Risk-adjusted	Multi-period	Captures flexibility
Real options	✓	✓	✓	✓
Decision Tree	✓	✓ ⊖	✓	✓
NPV/DCF	✓	✓	✓	⊖
EVA®	✓	✓	⊖	⊖
Earnings growth	⊖	⊖	⊖	⊖

BIBLIOGRAPHY

AA.VV. (1987), *Managing Innovation for Profit*, Technical Insights, Inc.

Albert, A. (1972). *Regression and the Moore-Penrose Pseudoinverse*, Academic Press, New York NY.

Amran, M., & Kulatilaka, N. (1999), *Real Options. Managing Strategic Investment in an Uncertain World.* Boston: Harvard Business School Press.

Arnold, R. (1995), *Strategic Management of R&D in the Pharmaceutical Industry*, BS770. Richmond, UK: Scrip Reports, PJB Publications.

Atkinson, S. & Wilson, P.W. (1992)," The bias of bootstrapped versus conventional standard errors in the general linear and SUR models", *Econometric Theory* 8: 258-275

Baker, A. (1998), "Pursuing the elusive goal of portfolio management." *Scrip Magazine*, 65, 46-49.

BCG (1999), "The Pharmaceutical Industry into Its Second Century: From Serendipity to Strategy", The Boston Consulting Group: *Industry Report.*

Bergstrom, P. & Lindberg, S. (1998)," Firms financial policy and labour demand. Theory and evidence". Working Paper, Department of Economics Upsala University.

Bergstrom, P. (1997), "On bootstrap standard errors in dynamic panel data models". Working Paper 23, Department of Economics Upsala University.

Bergstrom, P., Dahlberg, M. & Johanson, E. (1997)," GMM bootstrapping and testing in dynamic panels". Working paper 10, Department of Economics Upsala University.

Berk, K. N. and D. E. Booth (1995). "Seeing a Curve in Multiple Regression," Technometrics, Vol. 37, No. 4, November, pp. 385-398.

Berlant, D., R. Browning and G. Foster (1990). "How Hewlett-Packard Gets Numbers It Can Trust," *Harvard Business Review*, January-February, pp. 178- 82.

Black, F. (1993), "Beta and return", *Journal of Portfolio Management*. Fall.

Black, F., & Scholes, M. (1973), "The pricing of options and corporate liabilities". *Journal of Political Economy*, 81, 637-659.

Bode – Greuel, K., M. (1997), *Financial project evaluation and risk analysis in pharmaceutical development*, BS890. Richmond, UK: Scrip Reports, PJB Publications.

Bode-Greuel, K., M. (1996) "Project Management in European Pharmaceutical Companies". A survey.

Bode-Greuel, K., M. 81998), "Making wise decisions in pharmaceutical investments". *Scrip Magazine*, June 27-28.

Boehm, B. W. (1981). *Software Engineering Economics,* Prentice-Hall Inc., Englewood Cliffs NJ.

Bogner, W.C. & Thomas, H. (1996), *Drugs to Market: Creating Value and Advantage in the Pharmaceutical Industry.* Oxford, UK: Pergamon.

Bonsack, R. A. (1991). "Does Activity-Based Costing Replace Standard Costing?" *Journal of Cost Management,* Winter, pp. 46-47.

Brabazon, T., & Sweeney, B. (1998)," Economic value added, really adding something new?" *Accountancy Ireland,* 30, 3, 14-15.

Brealey, R., A., & Myers, S., C. (1996), *Principles of Corporate Finance.* New York: McGraw-Hill.

Breiman, L. (1995). "Better Subset Regression Using the Nonnegative Garrote," *Technometrics,* Vol. 37, No. 4, November, pp. 373-384.

Brigham, E., F., & Gapenski, L., C. (1993*) Intermediate Financial Management.* Orlando: the Dryden Press.

Brigham, E., F., & Gapenski, L., C. (1994) *Financial Management Theory and Practice.* Orlando: the Dryden Press.

Brown, B. & Newey, W. (1995*), Bootstrapping for GMM.* MIT.

Burk, K. B. and D. W. Webster (1994). *Activity Based Costing & Performance*, American Management Systems, Inc., Fairfax, VA.

Chen, S., & Dodd, J., L. (1997), "Economic value added (EVA®): an empirical examination of a new corporate performance measure" *Journal of Managerial Issues*, 9, 3, 318-333.

Cheser, R. (1994). "Kaisen is More Than Continuous Improvement," *Quality Progress*, April, pp. 23-26.

Chriss, N., A. (1997*), Black-Scholes and Beyond. Option Pricing Models*. London: Irwin Professional Publishing.

Clemen, R. T. (1991), *Making Hard Decisions. An Introduction to Decision Analysis.* Belmont: Duxbury Press.

Coates, J. B. (1976). "Tool Costs and Tool Estimating," *The Production Engineer*, Vol. 55, pp. 202-207.

Cochran, E. B. (1976a). "Using Regression Techniques in Cost Analysis, *Part 1," International Journal of Production Research*, Vol. 14, No. 4, pp. 465-487.

Cochran, E. B. (1976b). "Using Regression Techniques in Cost Analysis, Part 2*," International Journal of Production Research*, Vol. 14, No. 4, pp. 489-511.

Cohen, A., & Posner J. (1995), *A Guide to Clinical Drug Research*, Dordrecht: Kluwer Academic Publishers.

Cooper R. (1990). "Elements of Activity-Based Costing," in Brinker, B. J., ed., *Emerging Practices in Cost Management*, Warren, Gorham, & Lamont, Boston MA.

Cooper, R. and R. S. Kaplan (1988). "Measure Costs Right: Make the Right Decisions," *Harvard Business Review*, September/October, pp. 96-103.

Cooper, W. W., K. K. Sinha, and R. S. Sullivan (1995). "Accounting for Complexity in Costing High Technology Manufacturing," *European Journal of Operations Research*, Vol. 85, pp. 316-326.

Copeland, T., E., & Keenan, P., T. (1998a), "How much is flexibility worth?", *McKinsey Quarterly*, 2, 38-49.

Copeland, T., E., & Keenan, P., T. (1998b)," Making real options real" *McKinsey Quarterly*, 3, 128-141.

Copeland, T., E., Koller, T., & Murrin, J. (1995*), Valuation. Measuring and Managing the Value of Companies*. New York: John Wiley & Sons.

Cornelius, I., & Davies, M. (1997*), Shareholder Value*. London: FT Financial Publishing.

Cox, B. (1989)," Strategies for drug discovery: structuring serendipity." *The Pharmaceutical Journal*, 243, 329-337.

Cox, J., C., Ross, S., A., & Rubinstein, M. (1979)," Option pricing a simplified approach". *Journal of Financial Economics*, 7, 229-263.

Dahlerg, M. & Johanson, E. 81997), "An examination of the dynamic behaviour of local governments using GMM boot-strapping methods" Chapter III in Essays on Estimation. *Methods and Local Public Economics.* Doctoral Dissertation, Department of Economics, Upsala University.

Datamonitor (1997), *Drug Discovery Report*, London: Datamonitor Healthcare Reports.

Davidson, J. & MacKinnan, J.,G. (1993), *Estimation and Inference in Econometrics.* Oxford: Oxford University Press.

Davidson, J. & MacKinnan, J.,G. (1996), *The power of boot-strap tests.* Mimea Queen's Institute for Economic research.

Davidson, J. & MacKinnan, J., G. (1996)," The size distortion of bootstrap tests". Discussion Paper 937. Queen's Institute for Economic research.

Davidson, J. (1994), *Stochastic Limit Theory.* Oxford: Oxford University Press.

de la Garza, J. M. (1995). "Neural Networks Versus Parameter-Based

Applications in Cost Estimating," *Cost Engineering*, Vol. 37, No. 2, pp. 14-18.

Dean, E. B. (1985). "Finding Cost Estimating Relationships Using Principal Components Analysis," presented at the Seventh Annual International Conference of the International Society of Parametric Analysts, Orlando FL, 7-9 May.

Dean, E. B. (1989a). " Parametric Cost Estimating: A Design Function," Transactions of the Thirty Third Annual Meeting of the American Association of Cost Engineers, San Diego CA, 25-28 June.

Dean, E. B. (1989c). "Parametric Cost Analysis: A Tutorial," presented at the Second Joint National Conference of the National Estimating Society and the Institute of Cost Analysis, Washington DC, 5-7 July.

Dean, E. B. (1990b). "Perspectives on Weight and Cost pre-sented at the 49th Annual Conference of the Society of Allied Weight Engineers", Chandler AZ, 14-16 May.

Dean, E. B. (1991). " Modelling Personnel Turnover in the Parametric Organisation," Proceedings of the 13th Annual Conference of the International Society of Parametric Analysts, New Orleans, LA, 21-24 May.

Dean, E. B. (1992). "Parametric Cost Analysis or Let the Data Do the Talking," presented at George Mason University, 29 October.

Dean, E. B. (1993a). "Parametric Cost Analysis: Let the Data Do the Talking," presented at the 1993 National Conference and Educational Workshop of the Society for Cost Estimating & Analysis, Phoenix AZ, 21-23 June.

Dean, E. B. (1993b). "A Neural Network Expendable Launch Vehicle Cost Model," presented at the NASA Cost Symposium, Cleveland OH, 13-15 October.

Dean, E. B., D. A. Wood, A. A. Moore, and E. H. Bogart (1986). "Cost Risk Analysis Based on Perception of the Engineering Process," presented at the 1986 Annual Conference of the International Society of Parametric Analysts, Kansas City MO, 12-16 May.

Di Masi, Hansen, Grabowski, & Lasagna (1995), "Research and Development Costs for New Drugs by Therapeutic Cathegory". *Pharmaco-Economics*, January.

Dixit, A., K., & Pindyck, R., S. (1994), *Investment Under Uncertainty.* Princeton: Princeton University Press.

Dixit, A., K., & Pindyck, R., S. (1995)," The options approach to capital investment". *Harvard Business Review*, 3, 105-115.

Dodd, J., L., & Chen, S. (1996), "EVA. A new panacea*?" Business and Economic Review*, 42(4), July-September.

Draper, N. R. and H. Smith (1981*). Applied Regression Analysis*, 2nd. ed., John Wiley & Sons, New York NY.

Drews, J., & Ryser, S. (1997), "The role of innovation in drug development." *Nature Biotechnology*, 15, 1318-1319.

Efran, B. & Tibshirani, R.,J. (1993), *An introduction to boot-strap*. New York: Chapman & Hall.

Efran, B. (1979)," Bootstrap methods: another look at the jack-knife." *Annals of Statistics* 7: 1-26.

Eiteman, D., K., Stonehill, A., I., & Moffett, M., H. (1994), *Multinational Business Finance*. New York: Addison Wesley.

Elton, E., J., & Gruber, M., J. (1995) *Modern Portfolio Theory in Investment Analysis.* New York: John Wiley & Sons.

Evans, P. (1996), "Streamlining Formal Portfolio Management*". Scrip Magazine*, 43, 25-28.

Fama, E., F., & French, K., R. (1992), "The cross-section of expected stock returns". *The Journal of Finance*, 17, 2.

Farebrother, R. W. (1988*) Linear Least Squares Computations*, Marcel Dekker Inc., New York NY.

Ferrari, S. & Cribari. N, (1998), "On bootstrap analytical bias correction.*" Economic Letters* 58: 7-15.

French, M. J. (1990). "Function Costing: A Potential Aid to Designers," *Journal of Engineering Design*, Vol. 1, No. 1, pp. 47-53.

Geske, R. (1979), "The valuation of compound options." *Journal of Financial Economics*, 7, 63-81.

Godfrey, D. (1994). "Function Cost Models for Estimating Health Care Products Cost Baselines," *Value World*, Vol. 17, No. 3, October, pp. 11-14.

Gredenho, M. (1998), Bootstrap inference in time series econometrics. PhD Thesis, Stockholm School of Economics.

Greene, W., H. (1997*), Econometric Analysis*. 3rd edition. New Jersey: Prentice Hall.

Grey, S. (1995), *Practical Risk Assessment for Project Management*. Chichester: John Wiley & Son.

Gulledge, T. R. and L. A. Litteral, ed. (1989*). Cost Analysis Applications of Economics and Operations Research*, Springer-Verlag, New York NY.

Gulledge, T. R., W. P. Hutzler, J. S. Lovelace, ed. (1992). *Cost Estimating and Analysis: Balancing Technology and Declining Budgets*, Springer-Verlag, New York NY.

Hall, P. & Horowitz, J., L. (1996)," Bootstrap critical values for tests based and generalised method of moment estimators". *Econometrica* 64: 891-916.

Hall, P. (1992), *The Bootstrap and Edheworth Expansion*. New York: Springer-Verlag.

Harris, E., P. (1999), "An insight into strategic investment appraisal: project risk assessment". Doctoral Thesis—Henley Management College.

Harris, R. & Judge, G. (1998), "Small sample testing for cointegration using the bootstrap approach". *Economic Letters* 58: 31-37.

Harris, R. (1992), "Small sample testing for unit roots". *Oxford Bulletin of Economics and Statistics* 54(4): 615-625.

Hax, A., C., & Majluf (1983), "The Use of the Industry Attractiveness-business Strength Mix in Strategic Planning". *Interfaces*, 13, 54-71.

Hayes, R., & Garvin, D. (1982), "Managing as if tomorrow mattered." *Harvard Business Review*, 60, 71-79.

Henderson, B., D. (1973), "The Experience Curve Reviewed, IV. The Growth Share Matrix of the Product Portfolio". *Perspectives*, 135, Boston, MA: The Boston Consulting Group.

Holland, F. A., F. A. Watson, and J. K. Wilkinson (1974). *Introduction to Process Economics*, John Wiley & Sons, London, England.

Horowitz, J, L. (1997), "Bootstrap methods in econometrics. Theory and numerical performance". In D.M.Kreps & K.F. Wallis*, Advances in economics and Econometrics: Theory and Applications.* Cambridge: Cambridge University Press, chapter 7, 188-222.

Horowitz, J., L. (1992), "A smooth maximum score estimator for the binary response model." 60: 505-531.

Horowitz, J., L. (1996), "Bootstrap critical values for test based on the smoothed maximum score estimator". Department of Economics, University of Iowa.

Howard, K. & Sharp, J., A. (1983)," The Management of a Student Research Project", Aldershot: Gower.

Huchzermeier, A., & Loch, C., H. (1999), "Project Management Under Risk: Using the Real Options Approach to Evaluate Flexibility in R&D". INSEAD.

Imai, M. (1986). Kaizen: *The Key to Japan's Competitive Success,* McGraw-Hill Publishing Company, New York NY.

Iman, R., L., Davenport, J., M., & Ziegler, D., K. (1980)," Latin Hypercube Sampling". Technical Report SAND 79-1473. Albuquerque: Sandia Laboratories.

Islei, G., Cox, B., & Stratford, M. (1988), "Ranking, monitoring and control of research projects in the pharmaceutical industry." Lecture Notes in Economics and Mathematical Systems, 335, 191-202.

Islei, G., Lockett, G., Cox, B. & Stratford, M. (1991), "A decision support system using judgmental modelling: a case of R&D in the pharmaceutical industry". *IEEE Transactions on Engineering Management*, 38(3), 202,209.

Johansen, S. (1998)," Statistical analysis of cointegration vectors". *Journal of Economic Dynamics and Control* 12: 231-254.

Journal of Applied Corporate Performance (1994), Stern-Stewart EVA roundtable.

Kandebo, S. W. (1995). "Sikorsky Boosts Quality, Cuts Costs with Kaizen," *Aviation Week & Space Technology*, 1 May, pp. 39-40.

Kaplan, R. S. (1989). "Management Accounting for Advanced Technology Environments," *Science*, Vol. 245, 25 August, pp. 819-823.

Kenma, A. (1993)," Case Studies on Real Options". *Financial Management*, 22, 259-270.

Kerzner, H. (1995), *Project Management. A Systems Approach to Planning, Scheduling and Controlling*. New York: Van Nostrand Reinhold.

Kester, W., C. (1984),"Today's options for tomorrow's growth." *Harvard Business Review*, 2, 153-160.

Klein, R. S. and H. J. Tait (1971). "Faster, Better Tooling Estimates," *Industrial Engineering*, Vol. 3, December, pp. 12-17.

Kolb, R., W. (1997*), Futures, Options, and Swaps*. Oxford: Blackwell Publishers.

Kucher, E. (1997)," An International Strategy for Pricing and Profits." *Scrip Magazine*, 60, 30-32.

Kucher, E., & Hilleke, K. (1996)," A Practical Approach to the Pricing of New Products". *Scrip Magazine*, 51, 10-13.

Large, J. P., H. G. Campbell and D. Cates (1976). *Parametric Equations for Estimating Aircraft Airframe Costs*, The Rand Corporation, Santa Monica CA, February, R-1693-1-PA&E.

LeBlanc, D. J., J. Lorenzana, A. Kokawa, T. Better, and F. Timson (1976). *Advanced Composite Cost Estimating Manual*, Vol. I, Northrop Corporation, Hawthorne CA, AD-A041495.

Levi, M., D. (1996), *International Finance. The Markets and Financial Management of Multinational Business*. New York: McGraw-Hill.

Li, H., & Maddala, G. (1996)," Bootstrapping time series models." *Econometric Reviews* 15 (2): 115-158.

Li, H., & Maddala, G. (1997), "Bootstrapping cointegrating relations." *Journal of Econometrics* 80: 297-318.

Lillrank, P. and N. Kano (1989). "Continuous Improvement: Quality Control Circles in Japanese Industry", Centre for Japanese Studies, The University of Michigan, Ann Arbor MI.

Luehrman, T., A. (1998a). "Investment opportunities as real options: getting started on the numbers". *Harvard Business Review*, 4, 51-67.

Luehrman, T., A. (1998b). "Strategy as a portfolio of Real Options." *Harvard Business Review*, 5, 89-99.

MacKinnan, J., G. & Smith Jr, A., A.(1998)," Approximate bias correction in econometrics." *Journal of Econometrics* 85: 205-230.

Manski, C. (1975), "The maximum score estimator of the stochastic utility of choice." *Journal of Econometrics* 3: 205-228.

Marais, M. (1986), "On the sample performance of estimated generalised least squares in seemingly unrelated regression." Working Paper, Graduate School of Business, University of Chicago.

Maritz, J., & Jarret, R. (1978), "A note on estimating the variance of the sample median". 73: 194-196.

Matheson, D., & Menke, M., M. (1995), "Best Practice Decision Making in R&D". *Scrip Magazine*, 37, 34-37.

McFarlane, F., G. & Walker S.,R. (1995), "Portfolio Management in the Pharmaceutical Industry". Surrey: Centre for Medicine Research International.

McNeil, R. (1996), *Pharmaceutical Strategies*. London: Financial Times, Pharmaceutical & Healthcare Publishing.

McNichols, G. R., ed. (1984). *Cost Analysis, Operations Research* Society of America, Baltimore MD.

Meisl, C. J., 1990, "Parametric Cost Analysis in the TQM Environment", Paper presented at the 12th Annual Conference of International Society of Parametric Analysts, San Diego, CA.

Menzano, R. J. (1991). "Activity-Based Costing for Information Systems," *Journal of Cost Management*, Spring, pp. 35-39.

Mills, R., W. (1992),"Strategic Financial Analysis", *Treasury Today*, 2(12).

Mills, R., W. (1993)," Strategic Value Management: towards a financial framework for developing the general manager", *Journal of General Management*, 18(4).

Mills, R., W. (1994), *Finance, Strategy and Strategic Value Analysis. Linking two key business issues*. Lechlade: Mars Business Associates Ltd.

Mills, R., W. (1998), *The Dynamics of Shareholder Value. The Principles and Practice of Strategic Value Analysis*. Lechlade: Mars Business Associates Ltd.

Mills, R., W., & Turner, R. (1994), "Projects for Shareholder Value." HPW 9426. Working Paper Series-Henley Management College.

Moore, A. A, and E. B. Dean (1987a). "Estimating The Entry Research Vehicle," Proceedings of the Ninth Annual International Conference of the International Society of Parametric Analysts, San Diego CA, 5-7 May.

Moore, A. A, and E. B. Dean (1987b). "Using the MCPLXS Generator for Technology Transfer," Proceedings of the Ninth Annual International Conference of the International Society of Parametric Analysts, San Diego CA, 5-7 May.

Morgan, M.G., & Henrion M. (1990), *Uncertainty. A Guide to Dealing with Uncertainty in Quantitative Risk and Policy Analysis.* Cambridge: Cambridge University Press.

Moskwa, D. A. (1994). "Forecasting and Costing Technological Advances," U. S. Army TACOM, Cost and Systems Analysis Directorate (AMSTA-VCS), 27 July.

Nerlove, M.,L. (1998), "Bootstrapping—lecture notes". AREC, University of Maryland.

Newbold, P., & Bos, T. (1994), *Introductory Business & Economic Forecasting.* Cincinnati: South-Western Publishing & Co.

Nichols, N., A. (1994), "Scientific management at Merck: an interview with CFO Judy Lewent". *Harvard Business Review,* 1, 88-99

O'Guin, M. C. (1991). *The Complete Guide to Activity-Based Costing,* Prentice-Hall, Englewood Cliffs NJ.

Owe, A. (1988), "Empirical likelihood". *Annals of Statistics.*

Owen, D., L. (1983), "Selecting Projects to Obtain a Balanced Research Portfolio". In: *The Principles and Applications of Decision Analysis*, Howard, R., A., & Matheson, J., E. (Eds), 1, 339-360. Menlo Park: Strategic Decision Group.

Paddock, J., L., Siegel, D., R., & Smith, J., L. (1988)." Options valuation of claims on real assets: the case of offshore petroleum leases." *Quarterly Journal of Economics*, 103, 479-508.

Partovi, F. Y. (1991). "An Analytic Hierarchy Approach to Activity-Based Costing," International Journal of Production Economics, 22, pp. 151-161.

Peace, K.E. (1990), *Statistical Issues in Drug Research and Development.* New York: Marcel Dekker, Inc.

Pearson, A., W. (1972), "The use of ranking formulae in R&D projects." *R&D Management*, 2, 69-73.

Perlitz, M., Peske, T., & Schrank, S. (1999), "Real options valuation: the new frontier in R&D project evaluation?" *R&D Management*, 29, 255-269.

Phillips, L. (1995)," Prioritising projects and creating portfolios." *Pharmaproject Magazine*, Executive Briefing, August 1995, 1, 33-36.

Porter, M., E. 81987), *From Competitive Advantage to Corporate Strategy.* Harvard Business Review, 65(3), 43-59.

Putnam, L. H. (1977). "The Influence of the Time-Difficulty Factor in Large Scale Software Development," Compcon Proceedings, Fall, 6-9 September, pp. 348-353.

Putnam, L. H. and W. Myers (1992*). Measures For Excellence: Reliable Software On Time, Within Budget,* Yourdon Press, Englewood Cliffs NJ.

Rappaport, A. (1986), *Creating Shareholder Value. The New Standard for Business Performance.* New York: The Free Press.

Rilstone, P., & Veall, M. 81996), "Using bootstrapped confidence intervals for improved inferences with seemingly unrelated *equations." Economic Theory* 12 (3): 570-581.

Robinson, A., ed. (1991). *Continuous Improvement in Operations: A Systematic Approach to Waste Reduction*, Productivity Press, Cambridge MA.

Robinson, E. A. (1981). *Least Squares Regression Analysis in Terms of Linear Algebra*, Goose Pond Press, Houston TX.

Ross, S., A., Westerfield, R., W., & Jaffe, J., F. (1993), *Corporate Finance.* Boston: Irwin.

Salem, M. D., Jr. (1967). "Multiple Linear Regression Analysis for Work Measurement of Indirect Labour," The Journal of Industrial Engineering, Vol. 18, No. 5, May, pp. 314-319.

Scott, P. and M. Morrow (1991). "Activity-Based Costing and Make-or-Buy Decisions," Journal of Cost Management, Winter, pp. 48-51.

Seber, G. A. F. (1977). *Linear Regression Analysis*, John Wiley & Sons, New York NY.

Seber, G. A. F. and C. J. Wild (1989). *Nonlinear Regression*, John Wiley & Sons, New York NY.

Senn, S. (1996), "Some statistical issues in project prioritisation in the pharmaceutical industry". *Statistics in Medicine*, 15, 2689-2702.

Shao, J. & Tu, D. (1995), *The Jack-knife and Bootstrap*. Berlin: Springer Verlag.

Shim, J., K., Siegel, J., G., & Liew, C., J. (1994), *Strategic Business Forecasting. The Complete Guide to Forecasting Real-World Company Performance.* Chicago: Probus Publishing.

Shtub, A., Bard, J.F., & Globerson S. (1994), *Project Management. Engineering, Technology, and Implementation.* New Jersey: Prentice Hall.

Slater,S., F., & Zwirlein, T., J. (1992), " Shareholder Value and Investment Strategy using the General Portfolio Model." *Journal of Management*, 16, 717-732.

Smith, J., E., & Nau, R., F. (1995), "Valuing risky projects: option pricing theory and decision analysis." *Management Science*, May, 795-816.

Smith, K., W., & Triantis, A., J. (1995), "The value of options in strategic acquisitions." In: *Real Options in Capital Investment. Models, Strategies and Applications.* Trigeorgis, L. (Ed). London: Praeger.

Smith, M., C. (1991), *Pharmaceutical Marketing. Strategy and Cases.* Binghamton: Pharmaceutical Product Press.

Solnik, B., H. (1974) "Why not Diversify Internationally rather than Domestically?" *Financial Analysts' Journal* (July-August).

Stewart III, G., B. (1991), *The Quest for Value.* New York: Harper Business.

Stewart III, G., B. (1994), "EVA: fact and fantasy." *Journal of Applied Corporate Finance.*

Stockton, D. J. and J. E. Middle (1982), "An Approach to Improving Cost Estimating," *International Journal of Production Research*, Vol. 20, No. 6, pp. 741-751.

Stuart, M., E. Mullins, and E. Drew (1996). "Statistical Quality Control and Improvement," *European Journal of Operations Research*, Vol. 88, pp. 203-214.

Taylor, W. (1997), "Optimising performance through effective project selection and prioritisation." In: Practical Management Strategies for Maximising Productivity and Efficiency in Drug Discovery. Richmond, UK: Scrip Reports, PJB Publications / IBC Conferences.

Teisberg, E., O. (1995), "Methods for Evaluating Capital Investment Decisions under Uncertainty". In: Real Options in Capital Investment. Models Strategies and Applications. Trigeorgis, L. (Ed). London: Praeger.

Tippett, D. D. (1993). "Activity-Based Costing: A Manufacturing Management Decision-Making Aid," *Engineering Management* Journal, Vol. 5, No. 2, June, pp. 37-42.

Trigeorgis, L. (1996), *Real Options. Managerial Flexibility and Strategy in Resource Allocation.* London: The MIT Press.

Turney, P. B. B. (1989). "Using Activity-Based Costing to Achieve Manufacturing Excellence," *Journal of Cost Management*, Summer, pp. 23-31.

Turney, P. B. B. (1991). "How Activity-Based Costing Helps Reduce Cost," *Journal of Cost Management*, Winter, pp. 29-35.

Turney, P. B. B. (1992). "Activity-Based Management," *Management Accounting*, Vol. 73, No. 7, January, pp. 20-25.

Tyson, T. (1991). "The Use of Bar Coding in Activity-Based Costing," *Journal of Cost Management,* Winter, pp. 52-56.

Unal, R., L. B. Bush, J. M. Ball, and K. R. Lindgren (1993). "Aerobrake Parametric Optimisation Study," *Journal of Parametrics*, May, Vol. XIII, No. 1, pp. 51-65.

Van Giersbergen, N., & Kiviet, J., F. (1994), "How to implement bootstrap tests in static and dynamic regression models." Discussion Paper 7-94-130. Timbergen Institute.

Vose, D. (1996), *Quantitative Risk Analysis: A Guide to Monte Carlo Simulation Modelling.* Chichester: John Wiley & Sons.

Vrettos, N., & Steiner, M. (1998), "Quantifying the financial value of R&D." The Business and Medicine Report, May, 27-32.

Warr, W. (1998), *Strategic Management of Drug Discovery.* Richmond, UK: Scrip Reports, PJB Publications.

Webster, D. W. (1991). "Activity-Based Costing Facilitates Concurrent Engineering," *Concurrent Engineering,* November/December.

Weisberg, S. (1985). *Applied Linear Regression*, 2nd. ed., John Wiley & Sons, New York NY.

Weisman, D. L. (1991). "How Cost Allocation Systems Can Lead Managers Astray," *Journal of Cost Management*, Spring, pp. 4-10.

Williams, C.A., Smith, M.L., & Young P.C. (1995*), Risk management and insurance.* New York: McGraw-Hill.

Wong, K., F. (1996), "Bootstrapping human's exogeneity test." Economic Letters 53: 130-143.

Young, D., S. (1999), "Some reflections on accounting adjustments and economic value added." *Journal of Financial Statement Analysis*, 4(2), 7-19.

www.ingramcontent.com/pod-product-compliance
Lightning Source LLC
Chambersburg PA
CBHW030857180526
45163CB00004B/1614